WRITING MEMOIR

A Take-Action Workbook

Saugeen Publishers
Kitchener, Ontario

Copyright © 2019 by Heather Wright.

All rights reserved. No part of this publication may be reproduced, distributed or transmitted in any form or by any means, including photocopying, recording, or other electronic or mechanical methods, without the prior written permission of the publisher, except in the case of brief quotations embodied in critical reviews and certain other noncommercial uses permitted by copyright law. For permission requests, write to the publisher, addressed "Attention: Permissions Coordinator," at the address below.

Heather Wright
hwrightwriter@gmail.com
http://www.wrightingwords.com

Book Layout ©2013 BookDesignTemplates.com
Cover Image by Th G from Pixabay

Writing Memoir: A Take-Action Workbook
Heather Wright
Saugeen Publishers
ISBN: 978-1-9991038-2-8

This book is dedicated to all those who have given me happy memories.

When it was suggested that I write a memoir, I said, 'I'm not old enough. I'm not distinguished enough.' But I went home and sat down to write, and the material for the book just came flooding into my hands.

> Julia Cameron

I've yet to read a memoir by anyone I've known at all well that came anywhere near to the truth.

> Gore Vidal

Most memoir writers will tell you that the hardest part of writing a memoir isn't what to include, but what to leave out.

> Kathleen Flinn

Writing a memoir begins a process that doesn't necessarily end with publication. You begin to think about family life and stories and relationships, and those are ongoing.

> Sue Perkins

I was told that my best-case scenario would likely consist of writing my memoir and then disappearing.

> Amanda Knox

Contents

HOW TO USE THIS BOOK 1
WRITING PROMPTS TO INSPIRE MEMORIES 5
THE PEOPLE IN YOUR LIFE 13
THE WHERE AND WHEN OF YOUR LIFE 61
ORGANIZING YOUR LIFE STORY 73
      BRAINSTORMING PAGES 75
         FINDING YOUR THEME/FOCUS 75
      A LIFE IN THREE ACTS 79
CALENDAR 153
COLORING AND DOODLING PAGES 178
ABOUT ME 189

HOW TO USE THIS BOOK

You are already doing your research, reading the fantastic books out there to help you write your memoir. You have ideas, notes, reflections, information, and now you need a place to write them down. **This workbook is your desk-top companion on your memoir-writing journey.**

Well-designed tools created especially for writing memoir will guide your creativity and keep you inspired. And you don't have to work through this book in order. You might want to start with the process of organizing your ideas and then go back and focus on gathering the people-and-places details you need.

This workbook also includes journal pages where you can reflect on and celebrate your work plus a calendar to track your progress.

Use this book to schedule your writing time, beat writer's block with a little coloring, and best of all, get the words on the page as you've been dreaming them.

You can find out more about all my books at your online bookseller or on my website: http://www.wrightingwords.com.

If you find this book of value, **please stop by your online bookseller and leave a review**. I appreciate your time and your honest comments.

Other books in my genre-writing series–

Writing Prompts

WRITING PROMPTS TO INSPIRE MEMORIES

You have decided to write a memoir and that requires some digging into the past for those moments that you want to share with your readers.

Get out your laptop or journal and use these writing prompts to help you find the memories on which you can build your memoir. There are some extra pages at the end of this chapter in case you have some other memory triggers that you want to record and work on later.

1. Favorite summer memories—a picnic, playing with friends, a summer vacation, the beach, the plastic pool in the backyard, hide and seek ....

2. Think of the various doors in your past. Choose one at a time and answer these questions: What do you see and feel before you open the door? What do you see and feel once you are through the door?

3. When someone taught you to do something (ride a bike, knit, bake a cake, hammer a nail ....)

4. Your favorite hiding place

5. Best friend in grade school, high school, church, university/college, work

6. Stories your parents/grandparents told you about their childhoods

7. Being scared

8. Dealing with a bully/being a bully

9. Helping a friend

10. Helping a family member

11. Being alone

12. Lessons learned

13. Favorite teachers

14. Favorite aunts/uncles/cousins

15. Special vacations

16. Celebrations (Christmas, Hanukah, birthdays…)

17. Pets

18. Favorite—shoes, coat, dress, boots, skates, mitts, hat

19. Shopping trips – groceries, to buy a pet, to get new skates/shoes, to a different city

20. Best present ever

21. Describe the house you lived in/your best friend's house

22. Who were your neighbours when you were a child?

23. Describe your room

24. Describe your walk to school

25. Describe your walk to your friend's house

26. Your favorite subject at school

27. Your neighbourhood

28. What you wanted to be when you grew up

29. Your favorite pastimes: puzzles, drawing, dolls, action figures, cars, trucks, hopscotch, putting on plays, baseball, basketball, skipping rope, video games

30. Your favorite books or comic books

31. Your favorite games: outdoors—baseball, Red Rover, hide and seek; invented games; indoors—board games, cards, building a blanket fort

32. Rhymes for skipping and throwing balls against the wall

33. School trip or field trip

34. Favorite TV shows, radio stations

35. What you were ashamed of

36. What made you feel bad about yourself, your family

37. What made you feel proud of yourself, your family

38. What made you angry

39. How you travelled: bus, car, subway, bicycle, hitch hike. What model was the car? Color? What kind of bike? New/hand-me-down?

40. Favorite hangouts: roller rink, park, school yard, Dairy Queen

41.   Favorite music/bands

42.   How did you communicate? Pre-cellphone and WhatsApp, did you write letters, talk on the phone? What did the phone look like? Where was it in the house?

43.   Did you go to summer camp? What was it like?

44.   Did your family have a summer place near a lake or a beach? What are your memories of the cottage with your family?

45.   In your imagination, walk through your old house or cottage or your grandparents' house. Find a memory for each room.

Go back to your notes. See if you can add more sensory detail to the moments you remember—taste, touch, smell, see, hear. These details will help bring your memory to life for your reader.

NOTES

NOTES

NOTES

The People in Your Life

THE PEOPLE IN YOUR LIFE

Your life has been influenced, changed (for better or worse) by the people in it.

The following pages give you some space to dig more deeply into the important people in your life. Though writing a memoir means exploring your own life in detail, those that shaped you will be a part of your story, too.

Many of your impressions of those people will have been locked in while you were a child. As an adult, it's time for you to unpack these memories in the light of what you know now.

I've added notes pages after each worksheet. As you work on your memoir, you will discover more interesting things about these people by talking to others, reading letters, having pieces of your life's puzzle suddenly snap together in an aha moment you weren't expecting. These pages give you a place to record those inspirations.

NOTES

Person 1 _____

Physical description Job, hobbies, special skills	Background: parents, places lived, culture

Significant life event with long-lasting influence	Attitude toward life, family, friends

Goals, ambitions – achieved, thwarted	Fears, insecurities

How perceived by others	Key moments with you

NOTES

NOTES

Person 2 _____

Physical description Job, hobbies, special skills	Background: parents, places lived, culture

Significant life event with long-lasting influence	Attitude toward life, family, friends

Goals, ambitions – achieved, thwarted	Fears, insecurities

How perceived by others	Key moments with you

NOTES

NOTES

Person 3 _____

Physical description Job, hobbies, special skills	Background: parents, places lived, culture

Significant life event with long-lasting influence	Attitude toward life, family, friends

Goals, ambitions – achieved, thwarted	Fears, insecurities

How perceived by others	Key moments with you

NOTES

NOTES

Person 4 _____

Physical description Job, hobbies, special skills	Background: parents, places lived, culture

Significant life event with long-lasting influence	Attitude toward life, family, friends

Goals, ambitions – achieved, thwarted	Fears, insecurities

How perceived by others	Key moments with you

NOTES

NOTES

Person 5 _____

Physical description Job, hobbies, special skills	Background: parents, places lived, culture

Significant life event with long-lasting influence	Attitude toward life, family, friends

Goals, ambitions – achieved, thwarted	Fears, insecurities

How perceived by others	Key moments with you

NOTES

NOTES

Person 6 _____

Physical description Job, hobbies, special skills	Background: parents, places lived, culture

Significant life event with long-lasting influence	Attitude toward life, family, friends

Goals, ambitions – achieved, thwarted	Fears, insecurities

How perceived by others	Key moments with you

NOTES

NOTES

Person 7 _____

Physical description Job, hobbies, special skills	Background: parents, places lived, culture

Significant life event with long-lasting influence	Attitude toward life, family, friends

Goals, ambitions – achieved, thwarted	Fears, insecurities

How perceived by others	Key moments with you

NOTES

NOTES

NOTES

NOTES

NOTES

The Where and When of Your Life

THE WHERE AND WHEN OF YOUR LIFE

Even if you are writing about your hometown where you lived for 40 years, you are going to have to do some research. I know. I decided to write a mystery novel based in my hometown in 1965. I remembered where the Eaton's store was, but when did Sonny's Hamburgers open? Was it before or after 1965? If I want my main character to finish shopping at Eaton's and then go down the street to meet a friend at Sonny's for lunch, it had better be there.

Your library archives and old newspapers can be a big help here. If your town has a historical society, that's also a good place to check out. Scrounge family photographs and memories. Check maps, too. The old streets that you grew up with are likely the same, though in my town, the treed boulevards on some of the streets are gone to accommodate the growth of the city and its traffic.

How did you travel? Bike? Tram? Train? Bus? Car? Pickup? Foot? All offer sensory memories, too. People smoked in trains when I was a kid, and that's what that scratchy upholstery smelled like.

School yearbooks will help you remember what people wore and how they did their hair. Google can help here, too. There, you'll find lots of images from different time periods, some taken from catalogues. Movies from the time period might help, too.

Look for Top 40 lists for the time. What was playing on the radio? Your life has a soundtrack.

What movies did you go to? Did they smoke in the theater? What was your favorite snack? Did you go to the drive-in? Did you go to the fair or rodeo or circus or a major special event like a rally, a parade, or a concert? I remember the circus elephants walking down the street past my school from the train stations to the fair ground.

Did you go to a place of worship? What did that look, feel and smell like? Did you go to the library? In my case--old musty smell and scary librarians.

Were there any major weather or geological or wartime disruptions to life? I don't remember Hurricane Hazel, but my mom held me throughout the storm scared my dad wouldn't make it home from Sea Cadets.

Was your town under attack? How did parents react? How did kids react? How did you deal with loss? Having to move? Finding food? Safety? What are your sense memories? My mother remembers hiding under the stairs during air raids, right under the gas meter, and wondering why that was safe.

Use the next several pages to record what you do know about the places you will be writing about, list the questions you need to research, write down any resources, or draw any maps that you may need for reference.

NOTES

NOTES

NOTES

NOTES

NOTES

NOTES

MAPS & DRAWINGS

MAPS & DRAWINGS

MAPS & DRAWINGS

Organizing Your Life Story

ORGANIZING YOUR LIFE STORY

Here's the challenging part. How are you going to organize all your memories and ideas into a coherent story?

First, **narrow your focus**. Writing a detailed record of an entire life is daunting, and not necessarily interesting to your reader. Say, you are in middle age and have just found your voice, literally, by taking voice lessons and singing jazz in a choir. What led you here? What got in the way, so that you didn't embrace this amazing experience until you were 55? How has it changed you moving forward? Your story could be about how you found your voice. You now have your focus or theme.

Your second step is to **filter the events in your life through the focus lens** of *finding your voice*. If you focus on that journey, you will be able to select memories and incidents and people who helped and hindered that journey. You will find what changed in you to get you singing in front of an audience at 55. Now, you have a powerful framework for a memoir and one that others will identify with. Think how many other people long to find their voice. Think how many readers will identify with and learn from your story. *And this is why you don't have to be famous to write a memoir!*

Your third step is to **organize your story into a beginning, middle, and end.** I recommend creating an outline for your memoir before you begin writing, and some templates to help you follow this introduction. You may not follow your outline exactly. Things change. That's writing. But having a basic plan to begin with can be the key to getting the words on the page.

Unless you have limitless time in which to write, an outline will be your friend. You won't waste precious time staring into space wondering what to write about next. If the next item on your outline is a first-grade music recital that went horribly wrong, then that's what you write. Also, the outline helps you take advantage of short bursts of time to make progress on your story.

If you type at 40 words per minute, you can write 600 words in 15 minutes—roughly 2 pages! An outline also ensures that you will get some writing done on those days when the muse is on sick leave or sitting, sulking in the corner and refusing to come out and play.

BRAINSTORMING PAGES

FINDING YOUR THEME/FOCUS

Why do I want to write this story?	What have I learned that I want to share?

Looking back from now, what people influenced me?

Looking back from now, what events influenced me?

If this were a movie or a novel, what would be the turning point in my story?

Act 1

Here you establish the focus or theme of your story. Relate an incident that shows the origins of the challenge you work to overcome in the rest of your story. Introduce the people who, early on, helped or hindered your journey. Introduce your longing for *the something* that you will achieve at the end of your story.

ACT 2

Most of your story happens here. Moments of conflict, joy, revelation, humour. when relationships are frayed, broken, repaired, abandoned. Show how you faced the monsters and toughed it out. You may end this section with your lowest moment, then Act 3 will lift you to your success and reward the reader for staying with you.

ACT 3

Here you overcome that one last challenge and prove to yourself the value of your self-belief. This is not the time to preach about what you've learned but to share your insights as they relate to you. Show your readers by example. Don't tell them what to think. Your readers, who have identified with your story, will extrapolate their own meanings and lessons.

Journal Pages

JOURNAL PAGES

Here are 30 days of journal pages for you to record your progress through this book and through drafting your memoir. You don't have to write a journal entry every day. Maybe once a week will keep you on track towards your target.

Completing these pages will help you reflect on your process, determine next steps, and record any shiny, do-not-belong-in-this-project ideas that come to you while you're working on your memoir. I believe that you are most creative when you are already being creative. Ideas for a book about your favorite aunt, or a novel or short story based on one of your adventures, or a series of essays, all may come to you when you are working on this project.

And, when things get tough, or if you feel you are blocked, it's easy to want to drop what you are doing and go with the next shiny thing in your mind. I encourage you to acknowledge those inspirations, write them down, but stay focused and get 'er done!

Finishing is your best reward.

Date _____

The Step I Took Toward My Goal

_____
_____
_____
_____
_____
_____

My Surprises, Inspirations, Shiny Things

_____
_____
_____
_____
_____
_____

My Next Steps

To Do (research, word count goals, reading the experts ....)

Date _____

The Step I Took Toward My Goal

_____

_____

_____

_____

_____

_____

_____

My Surprises, Inspirations, Shiny Things

_____

_____

_____

_____

_____

My Next Steps

To Do (research, word count goals, reading the experts ....)

Date _____

The Step I Took Toward My Goal

_____

_____

_____

_____

_____

_____

My Surprises, Inspirations, Shiny Things

_____

_____

_____

_____

_____

My Next Steps

To Do (research, word count goals, reading the experts ....)

Date _____

The Step I Took Toward My Goal

My Surprises, Inspirations, Shiny Things

My Next Steps

___

To Do (research, word count goals, reading the experts ....)

Date _____

The Step I Took Toward My Goal

My Surprises, Inspirations, Shiny Things

My Next Steps

To Do (research, word count goals, reading the experts ....)

Date _____

The Step I Took Toward My Goal

My Surprises, Inspirations, Shiny Things

My Next Steps

To Do (research, word count goals, reading the experts ....)

Date _____

The Step I Took Toward My Goal

_____
_____
_____
_____
_____
_____

My Surprises, Inspirations, Shiny Things

_____
_____
_____
_____
_____

My Next Steps

To Do (research, word count goals, reading the experts ....)

Date _____

The Step I Took Toward My Goal

My Surprises, Inspirations, Shiny Things

My Next Steps

To Do (research, word count goals, reading the experts ....)

Date _____

The Step I Took Toward My Goal

My Surprises, Inspirations, Shiny Things

My Next Steps

To Do (research, word count goals, reading the experts ....)

Date _____

The Step I Took Toward My Goal

My Surprises, Inspirations, Shiny Things

My Next Steps

_____
_____
_____
_____
_____
_____
_____

To Do (research, word count goals, reading the experts ....)

- _____
- _____
- _____
- _____
- _____
- _____

Date _____

The Step I Took Toward My Goal

My Surprises, Inspirations, Shiny Things

My Next Steps

To Do (research, word count goals, reading the experts ....)

Date _____

The Step I Took Toward My Goal

_____

_____

_____

_____

_____

_____

My Surprises, Inspirations, Shiny Things

_____

_____

_____

_____

_____

_____

My Next Steps

To Do (research, word count goals, reading the experts ....)

Date _____

The Step I Took Toward My Goal

_____
_____
_____
_____
_____
_____

My Surprises, Inspirations, Shiny Things

_____
_____
_____
_____
_____
_____

My Next Steps

To Do (research, word count goals, reading the experts ….)

Date _____

The Step I Took Toward My Goal

My Surprises, Inspirations, Shiny Things

My Next Steps

To Do (research, word count goals, reading the experts ....)

Date _____

The Step I Took Toward My Goal

My Surprises, Inspirations, Shiny Things

My Next Steps

To Do (research, word count goals, reading the experts ....)

Date _____

The Step I Took Toward My Goal

My Surprises, Inspirations, Shiny Things

My Next Steps

To Do (research, word count goals, reading the experts ....)

Date _____

The Step I Took Toward My Goal

_____

_____

_____

_____

_____

_____

My Surprises, Inspirations, Shiny Things

_____

_____

_____

_____

_____

_____

My Next Steps

To Do (research, word count goals, reading the experts ....)

Date _____

The Step I Took Toward My Goal

My Surprises, Inspirations, Shiny Things

My Next Steps

To Do (research, word count goals, reading the experts ....)

Date _____

The Step I Took Toward My Goal

_____
_____
_____
_____
_____
_____

My Surprises, Inspirations, Shiny Things

_____
_____
_____
_____
_____
_____

My Next Steps

To Do (research, word count goals, reading the experts ....)

Date _____

The Step I Took Toward My Goal

_____
_____
_____
_____
_____
_____

My Surprises, Inspirations, Shiny Things

_____
_____
_____
_____
_____
_____

My Next Steps

To Do (research, word count goals, reading the experts ....)

Date _____

The Step I Took Toward My Goal

My Surprises, Inspirations, Shiny Things

My Next Steps

To Do (research, word count goals, reading the experts ....)

Date _____

The Step I Took Toward My Goal

My Surprises, Inspirations, Shiny Things

My Next Steps

To Do (research, word count goals, reading the experts ....)

Date _____

The Step I Took Toward My Goal

_____

_____

_____

_____

_____

_____

My Surprises, Inspirations, Shiny Things

_____

_____

_____

_____

_____

_____

My Next Steps

To Do (research, word count goals, reading the experts ....)

Date _____

The Step I Took Toward My Goal

_____

_____

_____

_____

_____

_____

My Surprises, Inspirations, Shiny Things

_____

_____

_____

_____

_____

_____

My Next Steps

To Do (research, word count goals, reading the experts ....)

Date _____

The Step I Took Toward My Goal

My Surprises, Inspirations, Shiny Things

My Next Steps

To Do (research, word count goals, reading the experts ....)

Date _____

The Step I Took Toward My Goal

My Surprises, Inspirations, Shiny Things

My Next Steps

To Do (research, word count goals, reading the experts ....)

Date _____

The Step I Took Toward My Goal

_____
_____
_____
_____
_____
_____
_____

My Surprises, Inspirations, Shiny Things

_____
_____
_____
_____
_____
_____

My Next Steps

To Do (research, word count goals, reading the experts ....)

Date _____

The Step I Took Toward My Goal

My Surprises, Inspirations, Shiny Things

My Next Steps

To Do (research, word count goals, reading the experts ....)

Date _____

The Step I Took Toward My Goal

_____

_____

_____

_____

_____

My Surprises, Inspirations, Shiny Things

_____

_____

_____

_____

_____

My Next Steps

To Do (research, word count goals, reading the experts ....)

Date _____

The Step I Took Toward My Goal

My Surprises, Inspirations, Shiny Things

My Next Steps

To Do (research, word count goals, reading the experts ….)

Calendar

CALENDAR

It can take a long time to write a book, so I've included a full year of blank calendars for you to use to track your progress. Since this book contains a collection of your thoughts and plans, it's a good place to record your word count or time spent writing or whatever you choose to log to keep you inspired by your progress.

Remember, writing in small pieces works, and you have the advantage of having spent time outlining your story. You don't have to wait for the muse to drop by; you know what you are working on next. And you can write out of order, too, if you like. If one scene is clear in your mind, write it, and put it where it belongs later.

Consider the numbers. If you write 250 words (1 page double-spaced) for 300 days a year you will have 75,000 words. Even if you only type at 30 words a minute, 250 words takes less than 10 minutes a day. I find these numbers encouraging—and they also take away the excuse that I don't have enough time to write.

NOTES

Month _____

Sun	Mon	Tues	Wed	Thurs	Fri	Sat

NOTES

Month _____

Sun	Mon	Tues	Wed	Thurs	Fri	Sat

NOTES

Month _____

Sun	Mon	Tues	Wed	Thurs	Fri	Sat

NOTES

Month _____

Sun	Mon	Tues	Wed	Thurs	Fri	Sat

NOTES

Month _____

Sun	Mon	Tues	Wed	Thurs	Fri	Sat

NOTES

Month _____

Sun	Mon	Tues	Wed	Thurs	Fri	Sat

NOTES

Month _____

Sun	Mon	Tues	Wed	Thurs	Fri	Sat

NOTES

Month _____

Sun	Mon	Tues	Wed	Thurs	Fri	Sat

NOTES

Month _____

Sun	Mon	Tues	Wed	Thurs	Fri	Sat

NOTES

Month _____

Sun	Mon	Tues	Wed	Thurs	Fri	Sat

NOTES

Month _____

Sun	Mon	Tues	Wed	Thurs	Fri	Sat

NOTES

Month _____

Sun	Mon	Tues	Wed	Thurs	Fri	Sat

Coloring & Doodling Pages

Image by Gordon Johnson on Pixabay

Image by Yousz from Pixabay

Image by Prawny on Pixabay

ABOUT ME

I always have more than one work-in-progress. I own too many journals, and I love red licorice, buttered popcorn, and chocolate–not together. I'm grateful for coffee shops where I can go to kickstart stalled projects. I love music, old films, and sing soprano in a choir. (Secret: I leave the really high notes for those who can land them without a squeak.)

I can't imagine my life without writers, watching them become motivated and empowered, and reading the great work that they create. As a coach, I love working one-on-one with writers of all ages. My current clients range in age from 15 to 90.

I am a former English teacher with 30 years experience in teaching English and Communications. I'm also a freelance writer, writing about everything from orchids to wind turbines to weddings to PVC pipe. I have written for national and local publications, and for educational publishers and industry.

My website, **http://www.wrightingwords.com**, hosts my blog and offers links to all my books for writers. You'll also find lots of free resources for writers of all ages and their teachers, too.

If you found this book of value, **please stop by your online bookseller and leave a review**. I appreciate your time and your honest comments.

www.ingramcontent.com/pod-product-compliance
Lightning Source LLC
Chambersburg PA
CBHW081356070526
44583CB00020B/2574